The Son of a Shoemaker

For Sally
With Best Wishes

Linda Black
January 2013

Linda Black is a poet and visual artist. She studied at Leeds Art College, Goldsmiths and the Slade, and has exhibited widely. Her previous publications are *The Beating of Wings*, Hearing Eye 2006 (a Poetry Book Society Pamphlet Choice), and two collections of prose poems: *Inventory* (2008) and *Root* (2011) from Shearsman Books. She was awarded the 2004/5 Poetry School scholarship, won New Writing Ventures Poetry Award 2006, and received an Arts Council Writer's Award in 2007. She lives in London and is a co-editor of *Long Poem Magazine*.

The Son of ~~an Apothecary~~ a Shoemaker

(after Constance Buel Burnett)

Poems & Illustrations

Linda Black

HEARING EYE

Published by Hearing Eye, 2012

Hearing Eye, Box 1, 99 Torriano Avenue
London NW5 2RX, UK
email: hearing_eye@torriano.org
www.hearingeye.org

ISBN: 978-1-905082-68-1

The poems are collaged from a fictionalised biography
of Hans Christian Andersen, *The Shoemaker's Son*,
by Constance Buel Burnett (Geo Harrap & Co Ltd, 1943).
The illustrations are original pen and ink drawings.

Some of the poems have previously appeared
in *Shearsman* magazine.

Many thanks to Bryan Angus at The Creative Retreat,
Gardenstown, Aberdeenshire – LB

Hearing Eye is represented by Inpress Ltd
in the UK – see www.inpressbooks.co.uk
Trade distribution: Central Books,
Hackney Wick, London E9 5LN

Design by Martin Parker at www.silbercow.co.uk
Cover image by Linda Black
Printed by Catford Print Centre, London

Contents

Nor the most prosperous   8

On Sundays his head was washed   10

Before he could feel frightened   11

For he was guilty of writing poetry   12

How did royalty talk?   14

She had grown used to watching his mouth   16

A stone's throw from home   18

Was he not already a little famous?   20

Whether the sun shone providentially upon
Copenhagen he could not tell   22

He had led many lunatics to the
Chief Director's Office   24

Many dancers are not at all handsome   26

His head swam from other causes than
mere suffocation   28

The sleeves were only a little too short   30

He was moved to comparisons of his
present struggles with those of the immortal poet   32

A very important vegetable   34

Under the stimulus of eager questioning
(she was no more than a portrait upon the wall)   36

The cord of ecstasy is a fragile one   38

The most exciting beliefs could be written in verse   39

Philologicum and philosophicum (with honours)   40

'Fra Andersen's saks springer eventyr straks!'
(From Andersen's scissors fairy-tales instantly spring!)
Hans Christian Andersen

In Memory of Hans Andersen,
Danny Kaye & my wonderful Uncle Cyril

Nor the most prosperous

Going without needed more but cared less. So far did his thoughts carry they often had to speak to him twice dependent on no one's hire. With hammer and needle and knife he could lay his hands far beyond. A rude wooden shelf contained everything out of the same piece of calico except on their backs the four shining plates spotless and tidy. Reverent fingers turned foolish dreams into small garments. (Her shiftless parents had driven her to beg nor a decent dress.) To be a scholar! Frustrated in boyhood (as from scorn) his mind under the rumpled blonde thatch was never meant. He broke the silence. She pushed. Indignantly for the poor little one he read aloud from the plays of Holberg.

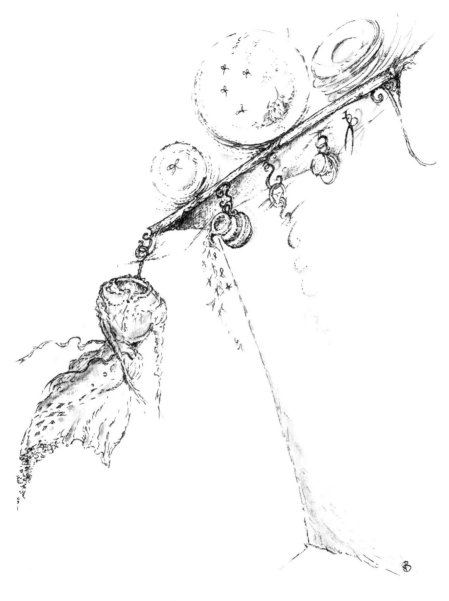

'A rude wooden Shelf....'

On Sundays his head was washed

The voice of new life curled against his index finger under its compelling influence. Ugly little face tiny waving fist cradled in the crook of a small trundle bed. *Thou art going to be tall.* Odd pieces of silk pinned across his breast to simulate a waistcoat as only a mother could. (His father and mother thought very differently.) She often took him to the asylum to play. While she raked and swept he outgrew. Then in she would don her one good basket enchanted and green-flecked and turn the key on her mountain which never seemed to diminish. But she was only a peasant.

Before he could feel frightened

Hans trotted the cobbles along his big mother's energetic stride. *Will the mistress have a rod?* Thirteen little girls and two little boys twisted round their benches. The chanting ceased. Curious stared. Wrinkled his ugly little face into a wistful: R-A-T rat H-O-G hog obediently joining. A rag doll slid close. A grandfather clock struck. Behind the mistress's chair two tiny figures danced out of a door and back shutting the door after them. It was several weeks later a sunbeam fell into the classroom. Glittering specks. Like fairies! Hans forgot. The stern rod came down whack.

For he was guilty of writing poetry

A-P-O-T-H-E-C-A-R-Y opened his speller. A clumsy young stork in wooden sabots sprouting about his clothes. Half-eyes slipped shut. Imagine living in a few moments ago! Unwise remarks stirred under the quilt. Several jumps ahead the king's fool arms protruded through dense clouds with amazing ease. A jester with a big nose. A good natured clay pig. If he did not walk carefully! Extra richness passed without further comment. Clattered in his presence for all the street to hear. To flavour the soup. *That* must be the reason. Life denied came forward: himself a Prince of Denmark with very long legs. *Come and see!* The strangest child encased in neatly darned stockings. Fru Bunkefold took the hat-box gently from him. She had heard of hunger of the soul.

'..The hat box...'

How *did* royalty talk?

His simple neighbours did not know. *Guten Morgen mon père har de godt sleeping?* (The princess spoke with dexterity thoroughly equipped to record the conversations of royalty.) The palace here for a fortnight! Agony of expectancy quivered on a footstool. *Thou hast a petition?* The August Presence before him went on flooding language with exacting diffidence. A penetrating glance set fire to the window. The stitching on the queen's cloak burst into song raspberry like a cloud. A tragedy of happy distraction. Just enough ludicrous little personality to bow himself out of the room. *If thy father were alive* flung out her wits. *Thou wilt have to swallow oil.* Alarm for his sanity emanated from the glowing hearth. To dance on a rope! In the middle of a pirouette he made a list. Twenty-five titles. Misspelled words never written. A cheap melodrama gesticulating and grimacing through the dimly lit streets in stocking feet.

'The stitching on the Queen's cloak burst into song....'

She had grown used to watching his mouth

One flickering memory nagged clear as a bell on the dresser if it were the silliest thing. The child must be saved! The cloth factory? Johann Hauch earned enough øres to fill two pigs all the way over. A small tobacco factory. He threw himself eagerly. To become a man! Coarse jokes called him a girl tried to pull off his clothes; crimson and perplexed his long body fled home. *Thou canst not work like other lads.* (Not the average son of a washerwoman.) Tremblingly alive with shoemaker's glue his small heart worked every evening over a grateful pincushion (the stitches had to be very tiny.) How much longer held out of what would become? Thoughts cleared her throat. *We must have a man!* The little room was very still. It was a large mouth.

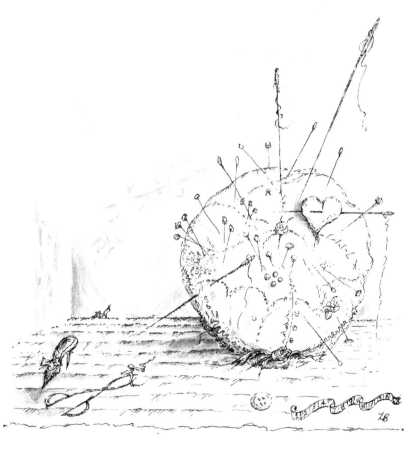

'... a grateful pincushion ...'

A stone's throw from home

The sprigged pattern left behind forever. (Ane-Marie's new shoemaker did not need it.) Eleven years! The shelf on which their lives stood still his father's books not unaware: shutting-out conveniently located in an attic room its narrow strip hurtling right down to the water's edge. (Whatever washing could be done easily.) Long twilight hours ran suddenly dry. Fish had been left. When the water gates were closed Hans could catch his hands. When the gates reopened the flood piled against his heels. A foaming cascade! The Chinese Empire lay directly beneath charmed by his distant singing. He had even drawn plans for the castle that would be his.

'The Chinese Empire lay directly beneath...'

Was he not already a little famous?

For three consecutive nights her tired brain jumped from the frying pan. Dropped unheeded in a glass of currant jelly shared with a sullen man. Scrawn and spindle clasped behind a crippled lap. Matters slowly growing. (If she hurried she would have time to cry.) It was not long before now Hans became an object. Nights slipped out unobserved scrambled into the wings his wide mouth fastened naïvely on the edge of the auditorium. Most in the world consisted of only one word. To seek his fortune. *Is it a monkey?* asked the Herr Direktor. How to save his white frilled shirt from the unforeseen? The boy must be confirmed. In the parish of St Knud his new boots creaked magnificently.

'His new boots creaked magnificently'

Whether the sun shone providentially upon Copenhagen he could not tell

A piece of glass no bigger than a tile inserted itself in a morsel of sky. His ancient stovepipe hat astir under the sloping roof awoke shabby and guileless: his thin body patched against wear and tear the day of days to begin. But it was a hat! Fru Schall would certainly be impressed. *You have talent?* A torrent of pent up boundings elated against the hard upholstery with spider-like agitation. Took off his boots. Lurched like an imbecile. Her porcelain gaze rose speechless from the couch. Cherry-coloured slippers famous for their ability wafted his great desire like thistledown throughout Europe. *Madame rang?* pulled a tasselled cord: the door silently open.

'.. pulled a tassled cord'

He had led many lunatics to the Chief Director's Office

You are much too thin said the Count. (A sentimentalist wisely not wasting any regrets.) A cure for aspirants totally unfit circled over the square. *Only during the month of May.* One brittle leaf pricked Hans' cheek coursed his face as much as to say what have you for me. A piece of cake? A large fish sandwich? His big hat (on its knees) stricken by his own temerity. Trees swirled past. Cheese and pickle filled the hot air. His mouth watered involuntarily: believed in particular applications whatever further calamity might befall. Nibbled a crumb. Like a spent bird under the nose of the astonished. It was not his fault that an hour or so later he became more interesting.

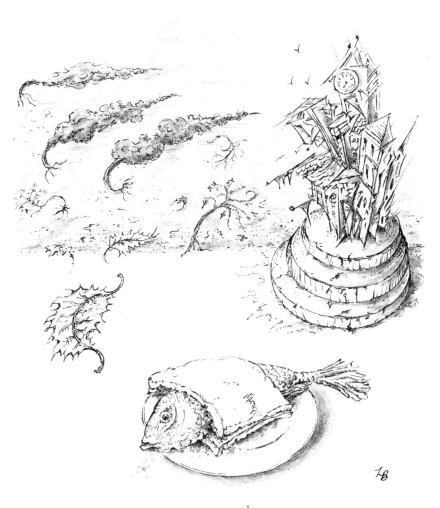

'a large Fish Sandwich..'

Many dancers are not at all handsome

Gaunt length hardened into angles the man he was to be.
All nose on incredibly big feet. The not distant future in
which he was to be famous swam with just such illusions:
began to do unaccountable things. *A little fun – nicht?*
Siboni tapped Hans' thin chest making the room ring. It
was his big bone structure. (He needed no make-up to
play the part of a troll.) *What to the voice happened then?*
Splinter-like legs drove both to the verge of frenzy quite
unintelligible to anyone but himself. No use thinking
shivered in the corner. Throat tightly closed. The world
would look different after soup.

'The World would look different after soup'

His head swam from other causes than mere suffocation

Great raw-bone hands cut with magic. Fragile lace. Paper-thin thighs. Mannerisms misfit and dilapidated. Gestures slipped and fell. Perpetual garments in danger of splitting held a pathetic maturity. (It was safer not to sit down.) *Hello bogie!* pounded down his throat arms rip-start and merciless. It was the half-grown world shrank as a beaten dog. He could not either avoid. Unwilling pity stirred the Singing Master: eyes sparked with strangely un-pedagogic amusement.

'Paper-thin thighs...'

The sleeves were only a little too short

There had been no stampede. (He took the manuscript wherever he went.) A human broomstick discreetly passed from house to house (before which the lorgnettes) ignorantly pushing into circles. Not a darn or a spot on the fine blue material. The next best foothold would appreciate the quality. How to fill out the depressions? (The present wearer could only boast a concave wishbone.) *So nice of you to come to see us this stifling day.* Strangely she had never seen a deformity before. (There was more than one hump). *Do unbutton your coat.* The pile of theatre programmes inside his chest crackled audibly. On the way back to his lodgings *I must be leaving* planned his next tragedy.

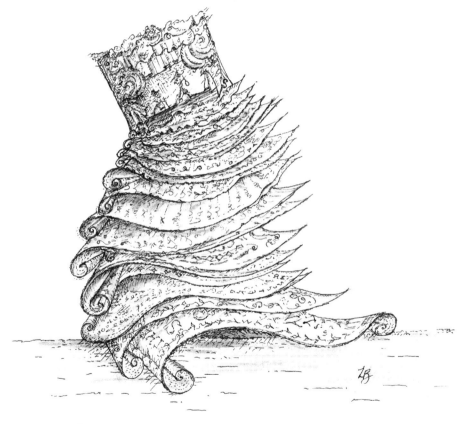

'The pile of theatre Programmes....'

He was moved to comparisons of his present struggles with those of the immortal poet

At exactly seven-thirty a caricature (three uneven sides) interrupted with immaculate irrelevance. (It was difficult for any servant to place such a visitor.) *I too have written a tragedy*. Whole sentences startlingly like sped in the direction. Fled unsolicited into a petrified cup. Behind an imposing coffee service the translator of Shakespeare into Danish hesitated: gold braid impeccable with censure. Pushed a plate of cold meat. (All human beings must eat.) One inch nearer: a few centuries to achieve.

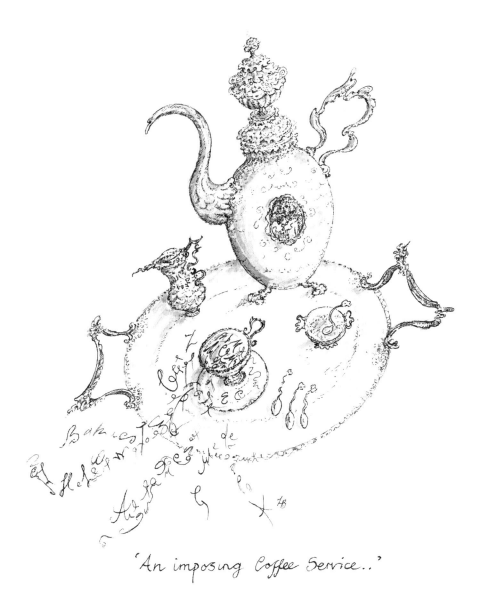

'An imposing Coffee Service..'

A very important vegetable

Eighteen twenty-three found him riveted on a herd of passing cattle. The podgy finger of learning all over again. *Wheat oats rye...* (Only the rustling grove could hear his prayers.) Meisling's soiled collar (no hint of brutality) twitted about his backwardness. To open the boy: great nose angular as a bird's beak... *barley root-crops haddock* ... a ship's mast above his classmates (the smallest schoolroom could throw him off balance) *oats barley rye...* A lungful of stale air (without feathers) bellowed impatiently. *Get him a brick to dry his tears on!* (There could be no real healing for the corroding affect of charity.) *Potatoes!* shrilled Otto gleefully.

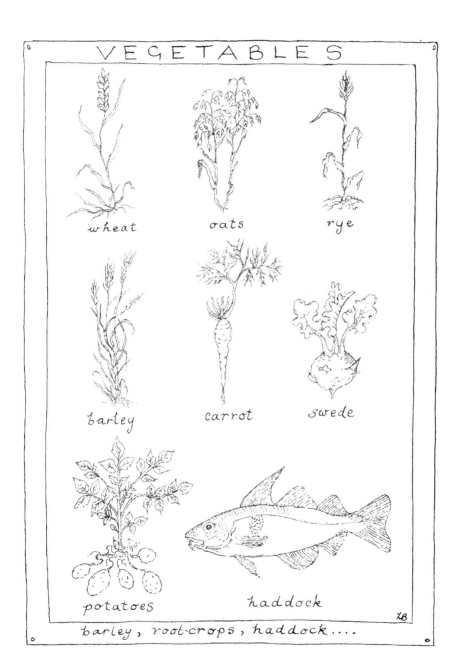

VEGETABLES

wheat　　　　oats　　　　rye

barley　　　carrot　　　swede

potatoes　　　　haddock

barley, root-crops, haddock....

Under the stimulus of eager questioning (she was no more than a portrait upon the wall)

Riborg smiled: *A cup will entertain you.* She led the way placed near a small table of books. Over her shoulder her voice stayed lifting its clumsy height: the top of her frilled pouring and passing. Hans trembled. Sweet oval framed the deft task. *From our own beehives!* He had said nothing at all which painted charm on his ugly face. Masculine stupidity came swift and intuitive: ungainly length brushed hers. Her eyes meanwhile! Covert glances unlocked another door of trivial things. For all they were absorbed in never far like deference a hundred fleetings must certainly have approached tormented by the necessity to know. The maid shrugged her shoulders. (She was able to talk quite connectedly about the weather.)

'A small table of books...'

The cord of ecstasy is a fragile one

Phantasmagoria picked him a nosegay. Rang easily and often his heart coiled against her braids: plunged him into that world less and less actual. To remain another day! Conventional greetings lacked her smile: melted in the pillared line of her throat. Filled the disturbing elements in him dissembling more than ordinary his own wound hurt. A fugitive in remoteness robbed of reality. Like a sleepwalker without volition the apothecary's son loomed in the background: grew as shadows lengthen.

The most exciting beliefs could be written in verse

A long blue reflection moved almost unnoticed. Impecunious and with tails. Mumbled incredulously into a piece of cake. More perplexing than any riddle of state he had never had to solve. Burning tapers cracked their whips. On trays in an upstairs room. Halfway-up a giant edition almost went to pieces. (An unconscious theatrical gesture.) A swaying rope. Carriages led astray. Prescriptions concocted out of inferiority. Footmen on snowy cloth valeting in deliberate disregard.

Philologicum and philosophicum (with honours)

Along the canals a filmy veil drew breath: coined words that could not know. Why *there* is one! Mercurial on the borderline spindling through the falling flakes. Quicksilver in a game of shadows. Patterns out of flux. Enchantment like a packed cupboard bewitched the marauding effects of himself. Came to him easily. He was twenty-five. Personifications lashed the Øresund. Scraps of paper fluttered like pigeons. Whirled his thoughts welter over his boyhood: ran the vein like a bright thread. Now that he was. The curtain began to cry *Author! Author!* Opened the door of fairyland.

'Personification lashed the Øresund'